LET'S FIND OUT! OUR DYNAMIC EARTH

WEATHERING AND EROSION

CAITIE McANENEY

Britannica Educational Publishing
IN ASSOCIATION WITH
ROSEN
EDUCATIONAL SERVICES

Published in 2018 by Britannica Educational Publishing (a trademark of Encyclopædia Britannica, Inc.) in association with The Rosen Publishing Group, Inc.
29 East 21st Street, New York, NY 10010

Distributed exclusively by Rosen Publishing.
To see additional Britannica Educational Publishing titles, go to rosenpublishing.com.

First Edition

Britannica Educational Publishing
J.E. Luebering: Executive Director, Core Editorial
Mary Rose McCudden: Editor, Britannica Student Encyclopedia

Rosen Publishing
Amelie von Zumbusch: Editor
Nelson Sá: Art Director
Nicole Russo-Duca: Designer
Cindy Reiman: Photography Manager
Ellina Litmanovich: Photo Researcher

Library of Congress Cataloging-in-Publication Data

Names: McAneney, Caitie.
Title: Weathering and erosion / Caitie McAneney.
Description: New York: Britannica Educational Publishing in association with Rosen Educational Services, 2018. | Series: Let's find out! Our dynamic Earth | Audience: Grades 1–4. | Includes bibliographical references and index.
Identifiers: LCCN 2017008750| ISBN 9781680488241 (library bound: alk. paper) | ISBN 9781680488234 (pbk. : alk. paper) | ISBN 9781538300268 (6 pack: alk. paper)
Subjects: LCSH: Weathering—Juvenile literature. | Erosion—Juvenile literature. | Geochemical cycles—Juvenile literature.
Classification: LCC QE570 .M425 2018 | DDC 551.302—dc23
LC record available at https://lccn.loc.gov/2017008750

Manufactured in the United States of America

Photo credits: Cover Barna Tanko/Shutterstock.com; p. 4 © David Mzareulyan/Fotolia; p. 5 Perfect Lazybones /Shutterstock.com; p. 6 © B. Kieft/Fotolia; p. 7 Matt Ragen/Shutterstock.com; p. 8 Martin Fowler/Shutterstock.com; p. 9 Kenneth Sponsler/Fotolia; p. 10 Anze Bizjan/Shutterstock.com; p. 11 think4photop/Shutterstock.com; p. 12 corlaffra/Shutterstock.com; p. 13 Galyna Andrushko/Shutterstock.com; p. 14 Denise Torres/Shutterstock.com; p. 15 © amarinchenko106/Fotolia; pp. 16, 21 © Encyclopædia Britannica, Inc.; p. 17 © Tom Blagden, Jr.; p. 18 Gary Ladd; p. 19 © Michael Fritzen/Fotolia; p. 20 pablo hernan/Fotolia; p. 22 © Corbis; p. 23 © MediaImages/ Getty Images; p. 24 Marco Maggesi/Shutterstock.com; p. 25 Chuck Place/Alamy Stock Photo; p. 26 © Ionescu Bogdan/Fotolia; p. 27 © Cole/USDA; p. 28 senicer/Fotolia; p. 29 © EcoView/Fotolia; back cover and interior pages background © iStockphoto/dmitry_7.

CONTENTS

Earth's Awesome Landforms

Have you ever seen a mountain? Have you ever stood at the rim of a canyon? These are just two of Earth's awesome landforms.

Vocabulary

Landforms are the natural features of the surface of Earth.

There are many different kinds of landforms. Mountains and volcanoes are high, rocky landforms. Valleys and canyons are deep cuts or low areas in Earth's surface. Harbors

Weathering and erosion by water and wind formed this natural arch.

Water flows down this rocky landscape. Over time, the flowing water will shape the rocks over which it runs.

and dunes are landforms along the coasts of oceans and lakes.

How are Earth's landforms created? They all start with weathering and erosion. Weathering is a process that happens when forces such as wind and water slowly wear down and break apart rock. Erosion happens when the wind or water move bits of rock and soil to new places. This movement changes the shape of Earth's surface, creating new landforms over time.

THE ROCK CYCLE

Weathering and erosion are parts of the rock cycle. The rock cycle is the process of rocks being formed, worn down, and formed again. The rock cycle doesn't happen overnight. It takes millions of years to break down and build up the landforms you see today.

There are three main types of rock. Igneous

This hot lava is starting to cool. Once it hardens, it will make new igneous rock.

This sedimentary rock is called sandstone. It's made of layers of sand pressed together over time.

rock forms when melted rock, called magma, cools down and hardens. The magma comes from deep within Earth. Igneous rock can be formed deep underground or when magma erupts from a volcano as lava.

Sedimentary rock forms from other pieces of rock. Weathering and erosion bring small bits of rocks together to form sedimentary rock. Finally, metamorphic rock forms when igneous or sedimentary rocks change under great heat or pressure.

Compare and Contrast

Compare the three types of rocks. How are they similar? How are they different?

What Is Weathering?

Imagine you're holding a rock in your hand. It would probably feel really hard, as if it couldn't be broken. However, many physical and chemical forces can break down rocks. That process is called weathering. Living things can cause weathering, too.

Over many years, weathering can shape rock into unusual formations. Weathering is responsible for many rock arches and hoodoos (lumpy

This weathered landform is made of slate, a metamorphic rock that was once shale.

Bryce Canyon National Park is famous for its hoodoos. The park has more hoodoos than any place in the world.

columns), such as those found in Utah's Arches and Bryce Canyon national parks. Weathering also has shaped the slabs of limestone in the Burren in Ireland and the formations known as the Pinnacles in Western Australia. Weathering can happen underground as well as above ground. Caves are formed by weathering of limestone rock. The formations within caves are also formed by weathering.

Think About It

Why are some formations caused by weathering smooth while others are rocky?

The forces that cause weathering are constantly changing. The landforms are therefore constantly changing as well.

Physical Weathering

Physical weathering affects different types of rock in different ways. Rocks are made up of **minerals**. Softer minerals, such as feldspar, are more easily weathered than harder minerals, such as quartz. Some rocks, such as shale, split and break easily. The amount of physical weathering also depends on the

Vocabulary

Minerals are solid substances that occur naturally and that do not come from living things.

This mountaintop is covered in snow and ice. Mountain weather can change greatly, causing freeze-thaw weathering.

When the water that collects in the cracks and hollows in rocks freezes, it expands. This is because ice takes up more room than water.

amount of time a force works on a rock.

Temperature plays a big part in physical weathering. When a rock heats up, it expands. That means it takes up more space. When that rock cools again, it contracts. That means it takes up less space. The movement in the rock may cause it to crack and break apart.

Temperature changes also cause freeze-thaw weathering. Water can make its way into cracks in rock and then freeze when the temperature drops. Water expands when it freezes. The ice therefore widens the cracks.

Chemical Weathering

Unlike physical weathering, chemical weathering involves a change in the makeup of a rock. Chemical weathering usually involves water. Elements in the water may react with the minerals in the rock. The minerals may break down or form different minerals.

Acid rain can remove rock by dissolving it. Limestone is a kind of rock that is easily weathered by acidic water. The rock forms cracks and holes. After a long time has passed, the rock

This photograph shows a close-up of holes in limestone that were formed by chemical weathering.

This cenote is in Mexico. The rock has been weathered away to reveal underground water.

may collapse, or fall away, and create cave systems. Limestone sometimes collapses, which uncovers water underneath. This creates cenotes, or deep sinkholes with a pool of water at the bottom.

Sometimes oxygen and water break down rocks and make them look "rusty." In other cases, acidic water breaks down rock into clay and salts. Acid rain weathers many different kinds of rock, and it can harm stone buildings and statues over time.

COMPARE AND CONTRAST

How are cenotes and caves alike? How are they different?

Biological Weathering

Biological weathering results from the actions of living things. These living things can be as big as a tree or as small as bacteria.

Trees can break through rocks if there are cracks in the rocks. The trees send their roots through the cracks in search of water. Over time, the roots will break the rock apart as the tree grows.

Bacteria, algae, and lichens are tiny

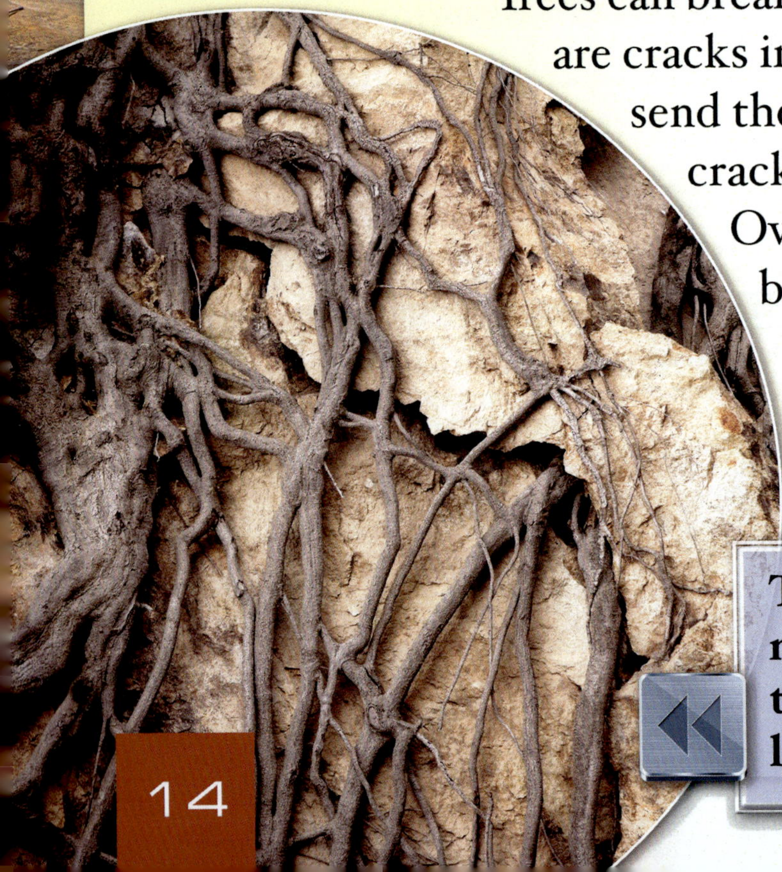

These tree roots are making their way through the surface of the rock that lies beneath the tree.

Lichens, like the orange ones growing on this rock, can survive in cold and hot places as well as in dry and wet places.

THINK ABOUT IT

Bacteria and lichens are tiny creatures. How are they able to make such a big difference in weathering rocks?

creatures that can break down the rocks on which they live. Lichens are creatures that are made up of fungi and algae. They grow on rock surfaces or within cracks. They may wear down a rock or carve patterns on its surface.

Some living things wiggle their way into rocks for protection. They can scrape bits of the rock away to get inside. They can also let out an acid that will dissolve the rock. Animals with these abilities include snails and mollusks.

What Is Erosion?

Many people think the words "weathering" and "erosion" mean the same thing. That's not true! Weathering is the breaking down of rock. Erosion is the movement of bits of rock from one place to another.

Types of Erosion

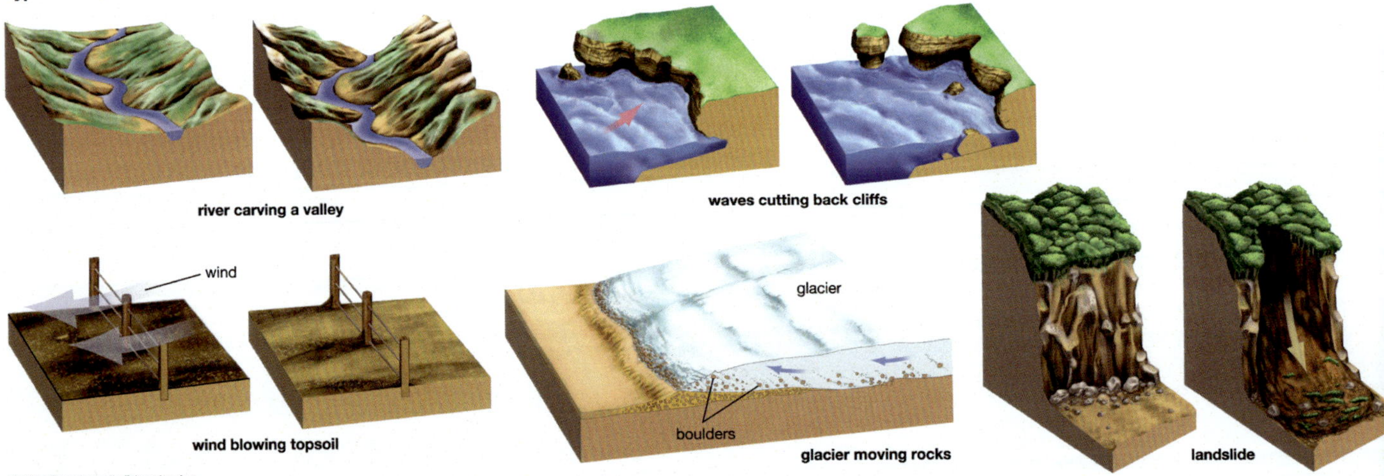

This diagram shows several different types of erosion.

Deltas are formed when a river splits into smaller rivers before reaching an ocean.

Water, wind, and other forces transport bits of rock and earth to new places. This movement changes the shape of land. A flowing river can carve a canyon over time. Ocean waves leave sand and pebbles on beaches.

Vocabulary

To **transport** something is to move it from one place to another.

Once a rock is weathered, erosion causes bits of it to be carried away. When the bits are left in a new location, that's called deposition. For example, a river may carry bits of rock and soil and then deposit them downstream. You can see deposition when you look at sandy beaches, sandbars, and deltas. Erosion, weathering, and deposition therefore work together. They change landforms and create new ones.

Erosion by Water

Water is one of the most common forces of erosion. River water picks up and moves rocks, pebbles, and soil as it flows downstream. These bits rub against the bottom of the river and wear away more rock and earth. This kind of erosion helped carve the Grand Canyon. The Grand Canyon is one of the most famous landforms in the world. It is located in the

The Colorado River carves a winding path through the Grand Canyon.

Think About It

Do you think the Colorado River is still changing the shape of the Grand Canyon today?

southwestern United States. Over millions of years, the Colorado River carried bits of rock and earth away from the land. This process eventually formed a huge canyon.

Ocean waves also cause erosion. The waves pound against the land. They constantly move pebbles and sand on beaches. The bits rub against each other and against the rock along the coast. Over time, the bits wear down rock into even more sand. The sand is then carried away by water.

The pounding of ocean waves turns rock into tiny bits of sand.

Erosion by Glaciers

Have you ever seen a glacier? Glaciers are huge masses of ice. Today, glaciers exist in only a few areas on Earth. However, there was a time long ago when glaciers covered much of the planet. Erosion from these glaciers created many of the landforms we know today.

How do glaciers shape the landscape? Glaciers don't just stay in one place forever.

Imagine how much sediment this large sheet of ice can carry as it moves!

Long ago, a glacier left behind this moraine in South Dakota. Moraine ranges from fine silt to huge boulders.

Vocabulary

Moraine consists of earth and stones carried and deposited by a glacier.

They flow slowly over the land. When they move, glaciers scrape away parts of the rocks and the soil below as they head down mountain valleys. They carry the bits of rock and dirt along with them. These bits aren't always small. In fact, glaciers can even move boulders as big as houses!

When glaciers melt, they leave the rocks behind. The materials that were transported by a glacier are called moraine. You can see moraine in valleys that were carved by glaciers long ago.

Erosion by Wind

Wind is the movement of air near Earth's surface. Wind can be a gentle breeze or a strong gale.

Wind erosion happens when strong winds carry bits of earth and rock, especially sand, from one place to another. In dry places, wind can carry sand into a big pile, called a sand dune. Over time, this sand dune will

Wind erosion formed these sand dunes in Death Valley National Park in California.

Arches National Park in Utah is home to many natural arches caused by wind erosion. The landform to the right is called Delicate Arch.

change its shape based on the amount of sand the wind brings and carries away. Wind also blows soil off of dry farmland. This is often bad news for farmers.

As wind throws sand and soil at rock, the shape of the rock slowly changes. You can see this kind of erosion at work in dry areas of the southwestern United States. Rocks seem to be oddly shaped because of many years of wind erosion.

Think About It

Why do you think wind erosion happens more in deserts than in rain forests?

Erosion by Gravity

Have you ever held a rock in your hand and dropped it? Why do you think it fell? The reason, in short, is gravity. Gravity is a pulling force. On Earth, gravity pulls objects toward the center of the planet. This is what makes objects fall toward the ground or down a slope. A landslide is a kind of erosion that's caused by gravity. A landslide is a large amount of earth, rock, and other material

This landslide in the Italian Alps is an example of erosion that was caused by gravity.

THINK ABOUT IT

How could landslides be dangerous?

that moves down a slope. Landslides happen when a layer of earth or rock separates from the layer below it. Weathering and erosion by wind and water can weaken the sides of mountains and hills. Storms and earthquakes can also loosen the top layer of a hillside. If the slope of the hill or mountain is steep enough, gravity will pull the loose layer downward.

This landslide in La Conchita, California, took place on January 10, 2005.

Erosion by People

It may surprise you that people cause more soil erosion than all natural forces together. This can cause major problems for the natural environment.

People tend to take over the land where they live. They clear the land to build homes, factories, and other buildings. They also cut down trees and plow fields to make ranches and farms. People also shape rocks to their needs. They blast holes through mountains to make tunnels for railroads and roads.

This section of a mountainside has been cleared of trees. This sort of deforestation leads to erosion.

Planting crops in alternating strips is one approach that can prevent erosion.

Natural erosion forces are not a problem. Soil forms about as quickly as natural erosion occurs. However, human erosion through deforestation and other activities is harmful. For example, crops depend on rich soil for healthy growth. When the top layer of soil is thin, wind and water can sweep it away.

VOCABULARY

Deforestation is the clearing, or cutting down, of forests.

Farmers use several methods to slow down erosion. They plant trees around farmland to block wind. They plant crops that add nutrients to the soil. They also cut terraces into sloping land to keep water from carrying the soil away.

Our Ever-Changing Earth

This river continues to carve its way between rocky slopes. A million years from now, it may look very different.

The Earth that exists today is slightly different from the planet on which you were born. Each day, rocks and soil go through weathering and erosion.

In the case of a landslide, the change in a landform can be very quick. In the case of a river carving a canyon, the change can take millions of years. Natural forces and human activities weather and move rocks and soil every day.

Compare and Contrast

You've learned a lot about weathering and erosion. In your own words, describe the differences and similarities between the two.

Do you want to learn about weathering and erosion up close? Visit a beach to see how the waves wash away bits of sand and rock and bring new bits to shore. Visit a canyon to see how rushing water could carve its way through land. Visit caves to see how acidic water has weathered the stone. Take a deep look at your ever-changing Earth!

These formations in South Africa's Cango Caves are the result of weathering and erosion underground.

Glossary

acidic Having or containing acid, a chemical that can break down substances.

algae A plantlike living thing that grows mostly in water and does not have true stems or roots.

bacteria Small, one-celled living things found in nature.

canyon A deep, narrow valley with steep sides and often with a stream flowing through it.

chemical A basic substance that reacts with other substances in a predictable way.

delta The triangular or fan-shaped piece of land made by deposits of mud and sand at the mouth of a river.

deposit Something laid or thrown down.

dissolve To mix or cause to mix with a liquid so that the liquid is the same throughout.

environment All of the things that surround a living thing.

gravity The pulling force between objects.

material A substance from which something is made or can be made.

mollusk A creature with a soft body lacking segments and usually found in a shell.

react To act or behave in response to something.

terrace One of a group of ridges made in a hillside to keep soil from eroding.

volcano An opening in Earth's crust.

For More Information

Books

Brannon, Cecelia H. *A Look at Erosion and Weathering*. New York, NY: Enslow Publishing, 2016.

Dee, Willa. *Erosion and Weathering*. New York, NY: PowerKids Press, 2014.

Hoffman, Steven M. *Weathering and Erosion: Wearing Down Rocks*. New York, NY: PowerKids Press, 2011.

Hyde, Natalie. *Earth's Landforms and Bodies of Water*. New York, NY: Crabtree Publishing Company, 2015.

Websites

Because of the changing nature of internet links, Rosen Publishing has developed an online list of websites related to the subject of this book. This site is updated regularly. Please use this link to access the list:

http://www.rosenlinks.com/LFO/erosion

Index